Finding Prospects

and

Generating Leads

Part Five

SALES TRAINING

Wayne E Shillum - Author

WES MARKETING

Finding Prospects

and

Generating Leads

Wayne E Shillum - Author

WES MARKETING

Dedication

This part of my Sales Learning Experience was
Perhaps the most Difficult
Because Prospecting is a Marketing function

For most companies the Instructions given were
"Get out there and sell"

With little or no Marketing provided by most of them it became
A DIY Trial and Error Journey

Here's to all the Sales Managers
Who forced me to become a Marketer as well

Table of Contents

Introduction

When the word prospecting is mentioned in general conversation we almost immediately think of the act of panning for gold. We see a person crunched over at the river's edge washing away the debris to find the glittering pieces of gold.

When the word prospecting is mentioned while discussing "***Direct Sales***" we often think of the following:

- Making countless telephone calls
- Knocking on doors (both household and businesses)
- Addressing and stuffing envelopes or sending large quantities of faxes or mailers (often called junk mail) to the marketplace
- The internet - emails, newsletters, blogging and social media
- Newspapers, Radio, or TV

Here too we are searching for the glittering pieces of gold.

Prospecting is The Marketing Attachment to Sales

We say marketing attachment because attracting prospects is what **Marketing** is supposed to be all about.

Marketing plans are designed to find prospects and use the best way to get the attention of potential clients or customers.

It is usually in a form of advertising to create a reason for the prospect to act.

Marketing is Finding Strangers

And Turning them into Interested Prospects

If done right, marketing should have a "*call to action*" that causes the potential prospect to contact your company.

When this happens, the role of marketing has achieved its initial purpose.

Once the prospect is attracted and a lead is obtained, the true function of sales starts to take shape.

Sales is Taking an Interested Prospect and

Turning them into a Buying Customer

Statistics show that approximately 80% of small to medium sized businesses do not have or use a marketing plan. They also do not have a marketing department of any significance.

That is why the responsibility of *"attracting and creating client interest"* has traditionally been left to the sales department in many companies.

The Sales Term used for this is *"Prospecting."*

Very often sales people do not take the time to learn and master the very important skill set of prospecting, that they have inherited.

The results are often very bad. Finding prospects becomes a nightmare and many people new-to-sales will leave the profession in frustration and disappointment.

Once Thing is for Certain

Prospecting can involve the highest amount of negativity in the marketing/selling process.

If an owner wants to obtain the most productivity from their sales department, there should be a significant company involvement in the marketing of their offerings.

When a marketing department does exist in a company, they will usually be responsible for advertising and promotions that will build the company image and attract prospects.

Many types of businesses take care of the total effort in bringing the client to the point of contact with the sales person.

While employed by these types of businesses, the sales person will have little need for being able to prospect.

Retail sales is such an example of no prospecting required by the employee/sales person. There are also many other types of direct sales companies that will also perform this task for the sales department.

What about the 80%

As stated earlier, 80% of businesses involved in Direct Sales have little to no marketing plans in place. They will leave the finding clients part, totally up to the sales department.

It is often a big mistake that is made by many businesses, not to get involved in the marketing/prospecting part of the process.

The owner will hire a sales person to handle both prospecting and sales and feel they are covered. They will have very little to do with finding prospects.

In doing this, many are placing the success or failure of their business in someone else's hands and fail to provide support.

The Reality is, that they have a vested interest in the success of their sales people and should participate wherever possible.

This part of our training has been written for those sales people who will need to find potential customers as part of their job and selling responsibilities.

It could be an owner or an employee who is the sales representative,

In either case; owner or employee, this skill set will be absolutely required for whoever is looking after the sales/marketing/prospecting for the business

Where Companies do get Involved

If two separate areas are involved (marketing and sales), finding clients should always be a cooperative joint effort.

There should be continuous feedback from the sales department to indicate what marketing is working and what is not.

- Left on their own, marketing does not always provide the sales department with qualified leads.
- If the sales department fails to communicate and inform the marketing department as to what is working and what is not, the problem of unqualified leads will continue.
- As a result, time is wasted by visiting prospective buyers who have no need or any real interest in a company's product or service.
- In some cases, the prospect will have absolutely no idea why the sales representative is there to see them.

Examples of how Bad Leads happen

Leads are often generated by a totally separate marketing arm in a company.

It often involves a telemarketing department and the telemarketer is looking to make as many appointments as they can get, to fill the daily quota set by the company.

The important step of fully qualifying the lead is left out by the telemarketer.

The sales department is sent on a wild goose chase, where there is no need or interest.

It also could be the result of a bad marketing campaign where the wrong message has been sent or the wrong market has been approached.

As a result, these efforts fail to provide quality leads for the sales department to begin their part of the process.

Conclusion

Therefore, sales people should have a significant involvement in the marketing process when it is done by the business.

This involvement will mean better control over the effectiveness of the company's efforts, to get qualified clients, and reduce wasted time by the sales representative.

Success in Selling Starts with Qualified Leads

The Challenges of Prospecting

One should never underestimate the challenges of prospecting. It takes a lot of effort and often very thick skin. It requires the knowledge and use of the first four parts of our Training series.

Part One "The Essential Elements"

This prepared you for the task ahead outlining all the ingredients needed for you, your company and your prospects. It provided the framework to handle Prospecting successfully.

Part Two "Qualifying and Closing"

This part showed you how to qualify your prospects and discover needs and how to ask for the order.

Part Three "Overcoming Objections and Conditions"

This part showed you how to keep going; overcoming the roadblocks and questions, from start to finish and to secure the order at the end.

Part Four "Meetings and Presentations"

This part showed the importance of communication and how to structure your sales Presentations.

These skill sets will be needed before you can successfully do the first part of your job in "Direct Sales" which is finding prospects.

The Basics of Prospecting

The Overview

Since 80% of small and medium sized businesses do not have a full marketing plan in use; it becomes the added responsibility of the sales department, to generate leads and find prospects.

Sometimes, the owner or sales manager will decide what form the marketing (prospecting) will take, and it becomes the sales representative's job to carry out their requests.

If management is not up to date on what works and what does not work; then you as a sales representative, may be asked to waste time on prospecting methods that no longer are very productive.

This Example is still being done

Sending sales reps out to find customers does not work if the sales representative is expected to develop a territory by making in-the-field cold calls to see prospects immediately

Knocking on doors, without appointments or previous contact is no longer acceptable by prospects.

Today, random cold calling without previous contact, is simply a "*Waste of Time*," if one expects immediate appointments.

However, cold calling and leaving information for Future follow up without asking to see someone, can be a very productive way to get started.

To the uninspired owner or manager of a sales department, the next may be one of the easiest instructions to give to their sales people.

"Get out there and make some Sales Calls"

"And get some Orders"

Cold calling is one of many prospecting methods that needs to be modified to suit today's type of purchaser.

Unfortunately, many companies will still send their sales force out to a very cold reception, resulting in poor to little success, and then blame sales for the poor results.

Random Cold Calling

This method will become a nightmare to find anyone who will immediately see you or be willing to listen. In addition, finding a company that has a reception area will be difficult. A telephone in the lobby has replaced most receptionists.

If there is a receptionist; the chances of being able to get past them to see someone, will be next to impossible without a previous appointment. Even getting a name can become an exercise in futility.

It will become very demoralizing for the sales person who is subjected to this type of prospecting, unless it is modified to suit today's purchasing practices.

Purchasers in the Business to Business (B2B) marketplace as well as today's Business to Homeowners (Consumer) (B2C) are no longer receptive to the old form of cold calling.

Outdated

In the past talking to random sales persons who were making cold calls, was how purchasing departments learned about existing and new products and services.

Now, they simply search for information on the internet and call the companies if they are interested. In some cases, they will make first contact because of successful marketing. (advertising or the branding efforts of a business)

If you use the old method of cold calling, you will not be very successful. If it becomes what is expected of you as a sales person, think twice about staying with that company, unless they will listen to other ideas.

Knowledge is Power

It is important to know what does not work and avoid these methods.

Today's Prospecting

Marketing methods are continuously changing and prospecting and attracting clients is marketing.

Other more productive forms of prospecting have now replaced the random no appointment "in-person" cold calling efforts for immediate appointments.

Once you learn these new and more productive prospecting methods, you will find it easier to locate your potential customers. This is when your actual real sales activity begins.

You will make the appointments, see the client and begin defining the needs or problems to solve. You will then prepare and make your sales presentations to get the order.

Some Changes Occurring

Many companies who are selling products or services still combine prospecting and sales.

The growth of social media marketing and other specific forms of focused advertising are now proving to be more efficient and cost effective.

When it comes to paying salaried sales personnel plus the added cost of their expense accounts to do both marketing (prospecting) and sales, there are good economic reasons for change.

Some companies have begun to separate prospecting from sales for better selling efficiency and for this economical control.

Effective Efforts

This can make the sales person more effective and productive by allowing them to focus on pure selling.

Unfortunately, it also has created a new problem of making sure that it is a team effort and the sales person is being supplied with ***qualified*** leads.

For our purposes here, we will outline the various methods available and leave it up to the company or individual sales person to decide who does what.

Whether it is called Marketing

Prospecting or Generating Leads

It has the Same Purpose

We are looking for Potential Business

Prospecting Objectives

In your search for prospects, there are the basic objectives that you will need to consider.

First Objective – Use the right prospecting method

Second Objective - Determine if there is a need and interest

Third Objective – Set your introductory appointment

1)Using the right Prospecting Method

Your success in this part will come from your research and learning about all the prospecting methods available. Certain methods will be better suited for your target market.

Your job will be to choose the right ones for your prospects.

We will be providing many ways to achieve successful prospecting results.

There will be Prospecting Methods

- That can be done only during normal business hours
- Some can be done in off-hours
- Some you will do completely on your own
- Others will involve people in your company or suppliers
- Make best use of your time and resources to achieve the optimum results that you can.

2)Determining a Genuine Need and Interest

This part of your prospecting will be looking for needs or problems to solve. This could mean finding more prospects doing the same types of things that your existing customers are doing.

It could also mean finding other uses for your products or services.

3)Setting Your Introductory Appointment

Once you have successfully completed 1 & 2 you are ready to set your first appointment. Use of your closing method *"Alternate of Choice"* is the best way to set appointments.

The Law of Numbers

The law of numbers could be loosely described by the statement: "If you throw enough mud at the wall, some of it will stick".

To undertake the process of prospecting (if it is to be successful) requires that you use the most effective methods known to your industry, to get your optimum results for obtaining leads.

Time, research, persistence and experience, will show you which ones to use and when.

After you have established essential traits required for a good prospect and acquired the necessary skills; the following is one example of the expected outcome as related to the law of numbers.

Telephone Solicitation Call Statistics

Out of every 100 predetermined eligible people contacted; normal results for telephone sales prospecting efforts will usually be:

- You should find 8 to 10 people who are interested
- Out of these, you should get 4 to 6 presentations
- Of these, you should get 1 to 3 sales

Once you know your potential market and the means of qualifying the prospects, you can rely on this rule or law of numbers (percentages) for certain prospecting methods.

Use the law as a base minimum to determine your prospecting efforts, and to set your own pace for the goals you have established.

Examples based on Law of Numbers

- If you want 1 - 3 sales, you need a minimum of 100 sales calls
- If you want 3 - 6 sales, you need a minimum of 200 to 250 sales calls

These examples are based on statistics when relating to telephone prospecting. Attitude, enthusiasm, and the right approach will get the results. Experience will increase your success percentages.

There will be a similar statistical outcome for any of the prospecting methods you will use. Once you find out what any of these methods take to get a sale, then you can determine what your efforts need to be for your sales targets.

When to Prospect

In this outline for Prospecting we will deal with mostly B2B (Business to Business) methods for your personal efforts. Most B2B sales persons will use the telephone to make appointments

Most B2C (Business to Consumer) businesses will utilize telemarketing or other forms of company related prospecting to obtain appointments.

We do not advocate cold door knocking for either B2B or B2C as an effective way to get in to see prospects if it is the first contact.

When Calling by Telephone

Choose a calling schedule that does not upset an existing or potential prospect. This means respecting the times of day when your prospect may be busy.

These busy times are Usually

- At the start of every day when people are getting organized for the work ahead
- At the end of the day when people are attending to the last-minute things they need to wrap up.

Note- The times shown below are based on a company with office hours that start at approximately 8:30am and end at approximately 4:30pm.

A Sample B2B Work Schedule

7:30 to 9:30 Use this time for traveling, planning, quoting, making promised telephone calls only. You can make in-person sales calls that have been previously arranged.

You can also use this time for Network Prospecting with your peers. (Perhaps an early morning coffee)

9:30 – 11:30 Use this time to do all types of Prospecting and it is prime time for seeing your sales appointments face to face.

11:45 – 1:15 Use this time to have lunch, travel, and work on quotes, summarizing the morning, planning the afternoon, or meeting your customers for lunch or your networking peers for coffee or lunch.

Note: Some companies do not look favorably on employees if they accept lunch invitations from sales people. Ask first if it OK.

1:15 – 3:45 Use this time to do all types of Prospecting and again is prime time for seeing your sales appointments face to face.

After 3:45 - Use this time

- To attend previously arranged or appointments requested by customer
- For summarizing your day's efforts, planning future prospecting, preparing of quotes and doing peer network prospecting.

Note: There is always a little flexibility in schedules and some companies may have different work start/stop times. Make the required adjustments to suit.

Work with the above agenda and establish your own time lines. Always respect your prospects time.

Common Courtesies

1) Each morning no new contact should be made before 9:00 - 9:30 to allow prospects to get their day started.
2) For afternoons make your last appointment start time no later than 3:30 so that you have enough time to complete it, leaving time for your client to finish their day. (unless otherwise requested by client)
3) On Fridays do not make appointments to start later than 3:00 PM.

Here we are showing *Respect* for the prospects time. No one likes to be approached with a solicitation call first thing in the morning especially Mondays.

No one likes to be approached after 3:45 especially Fridays unless it is important, or they have requested it.

Build Your Knowledge

Knowledge for Getting Started

a) Your Company and its Offerings

Find out everything you can about your company. When it started? Who started it? Who is running it now? Learn its history and how it has changed since the beginning

Most companies will offer some type of training for their offerings (products or services) and this is where you will concentrate on building your knowledge.

Find out what products or services you will be selling and everywhere their offerings are being used and why people use them.

Learn what all the benefits are, and where you are positioned in the marketplace regarding quality, price and performance.

b) Your Company's Marketing

Ask what marketing is presently being done by your company and the extent of any marketing plan that may exist.

- What they are presently doing?
- Do they have a web site?
  - How are they marketing the site?
  - Are they happy with its results?
- What Social Media Groups do they Participate in?
  - What are they doing in them?
  - Are they happy with the results?
- What else have they tried?
- What is planned in the next three to six months?
  - Can you participate in the planning?

- What are you initially expected to do regarding their marketing efforts?
- What support from them can you expect?

c) Competition

- Find out who your main competitors are
- What are their offerings, their benefits and weaknesses?
- Find out where they are positioned regarding quality, price and performance compared to your company.
- What Type of Marketing are they doing?

d) Customer List

- Get a list of all your Customers
- What products/services are they purchasing?
- What is their purchasing Volume per month/per year?
- Who is your contact? Their Manager? The owner?
- When did they become a customer?
- Why did they become a customer?
- Why are they still a customer?
- Have they recently had any complaints or issues?

Note: Do the above items (a - d) immediately upon being hired or you will miss the opportunity as a new employee to gather this knowledge with the company's blessing.

Starting to ask these questions after you have been employed for 2 or 3 months will upset your employer. They want to see new sales activity by this time.

Once you have completed finding out about your existing customers immediately continue with parts e and f). You can combine these calls with other prospecting efforts.

e) Appointments with Existing Clients

Make appointment and visit your existing customers as soon as you can and find out:

1. If they have any concerns or problems with your products or services?

2. If you can do anything to improve your services?
3. If there are any changes to office or plant operations, manufacturing, quality that are being considered that will affect your products?

In doing this research you will start building trust, respect and loyalty.

You will also:

- o Find out what reason may interest others in becoming a client.
- o Find additional business opportunities.
- o Obtain leads for new clients
- o Build your references list
- o Discover any areas of concern and provide answers to these problems.

Note: Your actions here could prevent the loss of that customer if nothing has previously been done to correct a situation.

Do these tasks as quickly as possible and do not make these meetings a huge project that might interfere with your quest for new business.

f) Establish your Prospecting Plan

One of the greatest areas of failure; as we have already mentioned, is "doing what does not work."

Many business owners or sales managers make the mistake of requesting prospecting methods of their sales department that do not work efficiently or even worse – do not work at all.

The further that people are removed from the actual selling activity; the more likely it is, that this will happen.

Requesting a form of prospecting without understanding how or why it is supposed to work will usually result in failure.

In this Part 5, we will describe many prospecting methods, so you can understand and decide what can be utilized best for your own prospecting efforts.

- Some will work well.
- Some work better than others.
- Some may not work for your offerings

It will be up to you to find where your efforts will be

This knowledge along with some type of analytics will usually show you which direction to take.

Always ask a new and existing prospect how they found out about your company; unless you made first contact.

Summary of Your Needs:

- Knowledge of your target market
- Knowledge of your products or services
- Knowledge of your company
- Knowledge of your competition and their offerings
- Knowledge of what works and what does not work
- Knowledge of Prospecting
- Knowledge of the Key Elements
- Knowledge of Closing
- Knowledge of Overcoming and Answering Objections
- Knowledge of Sales Presentations

Learn every type of prospecting and establish as soon as you can – what works for you and almost more important – What does not work!

Company Prospecting

Overview

It is best to totally get familiar with what the company is prepared to do in assisting your efforts to find prospects. The following are some of the ways that a company can provide help in the prospecting process.

Do not become discouraged if you find they presently are not using many of these methods as part of their marketing plans.

We are outlining them so that you can get an idea of what could be done. Your part will be to suggest adding them and finding ways where you can support their efforts.

You will also better understand how your input could be helpful in making these things happen or work better.

Clarification

For our purposes here, we are not offering readers an in-depth training of each method, but we are providing enough information to build awareness and to get one started.

Web Site

A company without a website is not part of today's business world. Web Sites have become an essential element in today's business world.

What a website does

It is a:

- Declaration that you are there and open for business.
- Focal point to send people to, for information about your company.
- Beginning of a company's branding process.
- Silent source of information for people to visit and learn more about the company's offerings.

You may have already checked to see if your potential employer had a web site in your job search. If they do have one, you have a base to work from.

If they do not have one, it would be a good idea to suggest getting things in motion to set one up when you are getting started.

How to get a Web Site Started

- Today you can secure a domain name and hosting for very little expense at sources such as ***"go daddy,"***
- User friendly ***"Word Press"*** is available on go daddy where you or your company; with a little training, can totally control the administrative duties at a very reasonable monthly cost.
- **Word Press** is easy to learn and use and will allow you to start with a very basic site without having a lot of web-tech experience.
- Go daddy also allows you to operate your own hosting services at reasonable rates. They are easy for the newbie and their technical support staff is excellent and always there to help.
- **Yoast** is a WordPress plug-in that you can add. It will help attract people to your site. It is easy to use and will provide basic Search Engine Optimization (SEO) features to attract the search engines.
- **Akismet.com** is a great source for controlling Spam and unwanted comments and it is very economically priced.

The biggest mistake that a company can make is to assume that having a website will bring business on its own.

"Build it and they Will Come"

This is often the thinking behind establishing a website. Just being there simply does not do the job of attracting prospects.

A website must be promoted to attract potential customers. A website without promotion is like having 1,000 business cards printed for your use, and then just keeping them in your desk drawer.

If your employer is unhappy with their existing website, ask how they are promoting it. If it is simply just there, the following are some ideas that will start building traffic to the site.

The following suggestions will get you started and provide the basics, if your employer will not agree to having a professional service look after this part.

How to Promote Websites (DIY)

If you do undertake the Do-it-Yourself (DIY) task to develop a website, it should be done after hours so you will not interrupt your prime time for your sales efforts.

Search Engine Optimization (SEO)

SEO traffic building is a slow process and usually does not get immediate results. Be prepared for this building process. Learn all you can about SEO in **Word Press** and **You Tube** tutorials.

Building Your Web Pages

With the free *"Word Press SEO plugin" "**Yoast**"*, you just need to follow their easy instructions to build your site's web pages so that they will start attracting the search engines and building traffic.

Start with their basic service. You can always add the more advanced levels later, after you are more experience and *up-and-running* for a while. There are also many other SEO plans on-line that one can utilize.

Company Blog (Post)

Again, it is a slow building process. Some statistics say you need 100 posts before any real results happen. "Yoast" is also a great tool for this as well.

Our Purposes Here

This section is not meant to train one "how to blog." It is simply to make one aware of these blogging features.

You will improve your blogging with persistence, time and experience and will see the results if you keep doing it.

Corporate blogs are often used to enhance the communication and culture within a company. They also can be used to express thoughts externally for marketing, branding or public relations.

Niche blogging can also be used to focus on a niche market of a company.

If no one is doing any blogging (posting information) on the company website, perhaps you might offer to start a blog. Base your activity on presenting your ideas and outlines to management for approval first, before posting them online.

Blogging is Free

Except for the time involved there is no cost and it will attract people to your site.

Once started however; it should follow a schedule and not become a hit and miss situation. If infrequent or scattered posting (blogging) happens, the would-be-follower soon becomes discouraged and will no longer look for your posts.

If you make use of your SEO knowledge and place the appropriate Meta tags and key words in your blog, you will attract search engines and people looking for information on these subjects.

Google Analytics is an excellent plugin for tracking

Provide an RSS feed link on you web page so that people can subscribe to your blog posts. Learn how it works, how to set it up and make it available. Word Press has great learning tutorials.

As you expand your blogging knowledge, you will find new ways to co-operate with other non-competing bloggers in your industry with promotions and extended readership.

Cards, Letterhead

Do not forget to have your company put your website address on all their cards, letterheads, emails, all advertising and every piece of correspondence that the company sends out (even shipping labels).

Wherever the Company Advertises and is Visible

The Website Address Should Be There

News Page on your Website

If you have a page for company announcements, upcoming events or new discovered uses for your offerings, this will build traffic.

Unlike a blog this page is like a news channel whereas a blog is more of an opinion source.

You can post your news letters on your web news page and archive them for anyone who wants to refer to previous ones. You can categorize them by subjects for easy search and find.

By placing general news from your industry on this news page you can develop a following of *"where to go"* to find out what's happening.

The buzz created will make you and your company an authority and bring new clients to look at what you might say or offer.

Paid Traffic PPA

PPA – Pay Per Action. Paid Traffic can be extremely productive. Before you begin your involvement in paid traffic, make sure you fully understand this activity and what attracts people to your site.

A lot of money can be wasted with no results if one jumps in and starts without enough knowledge of how this works.

Ideas should always be tested and split tested and proven at lower cost levels before up-scaling takes place. This will help prevent promoting a bad idea that could become very costly and end paid traffic as a type of prospecting for you.

"Google AdWords keyword tool." This is a great source for finding the right words and phrases to attract potential prospects. Use it for paid traffic or even on your blogs or website.

PPA (Pay-Per-Action). This is a general term and is where you pay to attract people to your site. The tools used are PPV or PPC.

PPV (Pay Per View) can be fractions of a penny and upwards depending on the subject and company advertising for you. You will pay for everyone who views your offer.

There are many companies offering this **PPA** service, so do your homework here as well. Remember you pay for viewing not traveling to your site.

PPC or (Pay Per Click) is more expensive, but here you pay only if people click on your advertising and clicking will send them to your landing page or website.

Make sure you have a great offer and call to action to turn lookers into buyers or at least provide names and addresses of prospects for your future follow up.

Offering to send free information or your newsletters when they provide their email address is one way to build a list of potential clients.

Do your research and start slowly to see what will work best for you.

PPA gets their attention and can start their journey to your site or landing page; but after that, it's up to your offer or advertising to make things happen.

Tracking of your results to see which type of promotion is working best for you is also available with these PPA companies. There are also independent analytical services to track your results as well.

Do your research as it is very important to have these ingredients working together in harmony.

Auto-Responders

Consider implementation of an email response service that will send your email messages to your list of prospects and customers. They can also automatically respond with information to prospects who provide an email address.

Make sure you are familiar with and follow the changing restrictions regarding the sending of emails.

Make sure the recipient has the option of requesting your email newsletters or advertising correspondence as well as being able to discontinue them at any time.

Most auto-responders comply.

The auto responders are usually very affordable and will look after a whole email program such as news letters or company announcements.

Two available services are: ***"AWeber"*** or **"Get Response"**

This could become an excellent source of handling and keeping in touch with all new and existing prospects for you. Email is very cost effective; especially if it is controlled by you.

Once you have your qualified lists, you can easily send out information to your prospects and existing customers.

No Time or Not a Technical Person

If you do not have the time to learn or you are not a technical person, there are many places available online that offer training and software to make your involvement easier and more efficient.

There are also many web development companies who will build your site and manage it. This can be expensive and may cause your company to question proceeding in the "web site promotion" direction.

There is no excuse for not getting started. If cost using a developer is an issue, offer to do this part yourself with input from your employer.

Get started as these services can always be added later

SEO Companies

There are many SEO service companies for you to choose from at several cost levels. This can be good if your company is willing to pay for these services.

If you want more than the basic SEO activity from DIY efforts, often it is better to have the experts look after this area and not waste sales time learning how.

Email Advertising

Emailing is still a very effective means of prospecting, if you have an accurate list of companies that are typically interested in your type of product or service.

Many people now have their email address on their business card; some companies may list a general email address on their web site or at least provide a contact form.

Most times a first attempt; if not requested by the recipient, can end up in the spam category. It is best to have a means by which the potential client will request information.

The "Call to Action"

Their request allows you to send without becoming spam

One way is to share promotions with other non-competitive people servicing the same marketplace with different products. You send their promotions with your emails and they do the same in return with their email promotions.

The restrictions have made the automated repeat email sending a little more regulated, and it has made it better and more effective for those who use it right.

Getting Permission to Send

Obtaining permission (the opt-in form or call to action) to send repeat items is good in this case.

Here the prospect provides their email address along with permission. Each item sent to them will also need a means to discontinue receiving them at any time.

You should have "an invite" to get your news letters or other free information placed on your site. Ask the viewer to provide their email address to receive either.

Summary

- Once they request your newsletters or information publications, you can continue sending them until they ask you to stop.

- Make sure you always have good content and helpful information.
- Give them a reason to call – a call to action as it is so accurately called.
- Provide an RSS feed link so that people can subscribe to your posts or social media site updates.
- With each email include a reminder that they have requested this information and have a right to discontinue at any time.
- The use of certain words in your headings can cause your emails to find the spam waste bucket.
- Learn which words to avoid using. Checking your own spam is one place to discover these words. *(Also google "Stop Words List" for more information on this).*
- The use of an analytical program can be very helpful in showing you what is working and what is not.
- There are excellent free ones with Word press and Google Analytics.

Social Media Networking

The term social networking is not new. The term has been used for over 100 years.

Social networking can be made up of individuals, organizations, or businesses that are connected by one or more specific types of common interests.

When the concept of social networking is used on the internet, it removes the barriers of time, travel and proximity. Your audience potential is worldwide, and contact is instant, unlike travel related networking.

Social media networking is a very useful tool for any company to attract customers.

Your company should become connected to the common ones and those sites relevant to their industry; so, they will be visible, and people can request updates and see them when they are posted.

Often social networking power will come from individuals at the center of the group's activity and is not necessarily attached to a level of management or authority in a company.

If you can become that center and authority in your company, your peers and prospects will respect and trust you.

Some Main Sites

- FACEBOOK
- TWITTER
- LINKEDIN

There are many choices, so do your research. Find the ones best suited for your company and keep your involvement consistent.

Once Involved

Your company will have a chance on each to build a profile. Link back to the business web site if terms and conditions allow.

Use their business functions to attract potential prospects. These social sites are great prospecting tools and should be utilized.

Consider doing it yourself if your company is not involved

Often there are discussion groups on sites such as LinkedIn that may offer an opportunity to reach your target market. Get involved and get your message out there.

Look for sites that relate to your offerings and join them. You should get permission from your employer if you are promoting your company on them.

If you are doing it as a personal exposure vehicle on your own, you will probably not need to get permission, but it is still a good idea to at least inform them.

Trade Shows - as an Exhibitor

An excellent source of leads can be obtained by being an exhibitor at trade shows. The biggest drawback to this type of prospecting for your employer is that, shows tend to be expensive.

Trade shows make it very easy to spend dollars on gadgets and gimmicks and other things that have little or no effect on your overall results.

Experience will help reduce these costs considerably and improve the shows ROI (Return on Investment). Encourage your company to participate in such events.

Many companies (potential prospects) attend shows to secure information for their purchasing.

Companies often send people who will be involved in decision making for any upcoming projects or find new sources for their existing needs.

Trade Show Tips

One of the factors to make trade shows a success is to be an active and receptive person.

Bring lots of simple but well-designed advertising aids to hand out.

Always have someone standing out front and greeting people as they go by. Sitting in the back of your booth and waiting for people to come to you is not very effective.

Be enthusiastic and friendly when handing out information. This will demonstrate how well you would service your potential prospect should they become a customer.

Take names and get their business cards and ask for email addresses.

The people who just display promotional material, and sit back, expecting the visitors to take the initiative; will leave the prospect with a negative feeling.

They may think that they are now experiencing the level of service they can expect from that supplier.

Other Benefits of Trade Shows

- Another asset in being an exhibitor in trade shows is the image-building you receive by interacting with potential customers, and the involvement with your peer group.
- You and your employer become a visible and important part of your industry.
- It gives you the chance to network from the prestigious level of a Trade Show exhibitor.
- Often these shows will provide the possibility of putting on a seminar about your products or services. This is a great avenue for providing exposure and building trust in your company.

Become a leader in your industry and someone that your clients will look up to as an authority on the products or services that you are promoting.

Telemarketing

If your company has any number of outside sales representatives, it may also have a telemarketing department to arrange calls for their sales representatives.

This allows the sales representative to devote more time to pure selling.

Cost Effective

With the increasing costs for gas, the travel time along with the ineffectiveness of cold prospecting, many companies have or are considering telemarketing to lower their overall lead gathering costs.

Cold telephone calling in the form of prospecting, is often something that many sales representatives who are on the road hate to do anyway.

Personally, I found making telephone calls myself, to be a very effective prospecting method. Provided I started with a pre-selected group selected by myself, the results were very productive.

Areas of Caution

Leads produced for the sake of the telemarketer getting the required appointment numbers, can become a real danger.

It is important for you as a sales representative to be able to follow up and qualify the lead, confirm the interest and appointment, re-set it or cancel it. Qualification increases efficiency and closing ratios.

If your employer has telemarketing in place, make sure you have a way to provide feedback on the quality of leads you are getting. Your input into what you are looking for in a prospect is essential.

Make this involvement part of your sales agenda or you may find that you are too often involved in the proverbial wild goose chase.

Direct Mail

Direct Mail is the type of mail that is sent to very specific people and companies. It involves addressing and stuffing envelopes and applying postage.

Use a good source for recipient company information and up-to-date employee contact names. There are many Trade and Business Directories available online and at local libraries.

Be Specific

This is not a mass mailing as postage is involved, and you should be very specific about the type of company and people you are sending your direct mail to.

There are sources and programs that will allow you to choose the main parameters of your search and even print labels of all the companies found.

Unless you streamline your selection process, and choose your target market carefully, your approach may be too general. It will produce mediocre results and it can become very costly.

If not done correctly your company could look at the Return on Investment (ROI) and feel that it is too expensive to continue.

Once you have the experience in identifying good potential prospects, go through these lists and select the type of company, and the level of management that you want to receive this information.

The selection part of these companies and names is best done by you and works well for your "Off hour Prospecting"

Company Assistance

Give these lists to a secretary in your company to address each envelope, add the information, apply postage, and send the letter directly to the people you have chosen.

Make sure a list of names and telephone numbers has been made and is available for follow up.

You can assist by stuffing the envelopes after hours. It is a satisfying way to create the feeling of teamwork, if you show appreciation to the others involved.

Keep the Information Simple and to the Point

Too many Words - Will go right to the Trash

Direct mail is a great method to provide extra prospecting capabilities, without taking time from the most productive part of your day which is 9:00 to 5:00 for making appointments and seeing your potential customers.

Time Consuming

Direct mail is a time-consuming method, and what better time than after hours to establish your list of potential prospects.

Make time for a small amount to be done each day/week. Small daily or weekly mailings will hardly be noticed.

This applies to your office help and applies to the cost factor.

It also will create leads on a steady pace that you can handle.

Set your goals and stick to them. After a short time, you will see the results with increased inquires.

The Follow Up

Use your list of the places you have sent this information to c/w names and telephone numbers. Wait 3 or 4 days and follow up with a phone call. Smaller mailings will make this easier and more efficient.

News Letters

If your employer is not actively involved in any kind of newsletter, start doing one yourself (with permission). We have outlined information in the section "Personal Prospecting."

Mass Mailing - No Name - No Address

If your company has a product that is widely used or multiple products, this can work well as a third level prospecting method.

This was something I did, when nothing else seemed to be working.

It would also produce leads from the most unsuspecting areas. That is why I used it. Keep the mailings controlled from a cost standpoint. Bi-weekly or Monthly mailings are far better than one huge mailing.

What works?

This also gives one a chance to see what is working and what is not. There is no telephone follow up here

Over the years, I found that dumping a huge quantity of this type on the marketplace at once; whatever the delivery service was, did not produce very good results.

It often seemed like the larger the quantity was; that I sent out, the lower the percentage of results.

Releasing mailers in smaller quantities over a longer time span seemed to increase the success levels in the response factor.

The Downside to this Type

Unfortunately, mail without a name and stamp, is often treated as junk and often does not reach its intended destination.

There is no accountability by anyone and most people know it. We have also all heard the stories of huge quantities of mailers found in dumpsters that were never delivered.

The overall results and the ROI per new customer obtained will determine if this method makes any sense to your company.

Choose a reliable delivery source and make sure your information shows your website's address company telephone number and your email address.

Most importantly, it must have a good call to action or offer.

Do random checks for delivery and let your delivery source know you will be doing them. After all, you are paying them to deliver your mailers and it will defiantly increase the delivery rate and your return.

Paid Media

Paid media can become very costly and not all will work for your employer's offerings. Tread very lightly before you suggest any of them.

Usually a good sign of their effectiveness might be if your competition is using one or more of them.

In the following areas, we suggest that you do your research and obtain the advertising costs. Also, find out the advertising strategies attached to each method.

Do this in non-prime-time for prospecting. Fully put together the results on your own before you start suggesting the use of any.

Find out what the benefits are for each and why the source feels their method would work for you.

Newspapers

Call or visit your local newspapers and ask for their advertising rates. They will usually have a package outlining everything you would need.

Their reach will also usually include other newspaper groups that they are involved with, outside of your community. You can usually pick and choose the communities you want to reach, by selecting these other groups individually.

Trade Magazines

This can be a very effective form of advertising if the magazine is focused on your industry. If it is a good source, there will be many competitors there as well.

Study the magazines for several issues and see what is being done. Make sure that whatever you do looks equal to, or better than your competition. You will immediately be judged on what you do because you are a new player.

Have Quality Content and a good Call to Action

Radio and TV

Contact your local radio and TV stations and ask for an advertising portfolio for small business.

Find out what support they would provide in putting a campaign together for you. Even if you feel you would not use these sources, knowledge is the best way to make your decisions.

Bill Boards

Often bill boards will work for a short period of time. After a while they can just become part of the scenery background. Changing information on them periodically or changing location, can reduce this "blending-in" aspect.

Mobile Cards

If you are part of a larger community where they have taxis, buses, park benches or benches at transit stops, you will often see this type of advertising.

Often it is used by professionals such as real estate agents or by businesses offering products or services to consumers.

Webinars

The term webinar is a short form for a web-based Seminar. It can be a presentation, lecture, workshop or seminar that is transmitted over the web through a host.

There is usually notification and a sign-up process with the time and access information sent to the email address of the participants.

Prospects will view the activity on their computer screen and in most cases, they will listen with the speakers connected to their computer. Usually they have an option to use a telephone for audio.

Live or Recorded

Webinars can either be live presentations or previously formatted and recorded for viewing or listening.

Often there will be a live chat line for questions and responses to various parts of the webinar presentation.

If the webinar has been recorded, you or your company can use it for repeat broadcasts or convenient viewing in different time zones or to suit the schedules of the recipients.

Placing your past recorded webinars on your website, can provide a continuous source of prospect attraction. They can also become great background attention aids at trade shows.

If the company is not involved in any kind of webinar activity, suggest starting with a trial webinar and if successful build it into a bi-monthly or monthly activity.

Open House

One way of building relations with your clients as well as attracting new ones is to have open house demonstrations of your products and services.

Have your internal office staff participate. Keep it informal to create a comfort level with the people attending.

Presentations to Organisations

There are many opportunities that exist in local organizations or groups doing promotions or holding events.

Look for ones that could assist in your company's exposure. You could offer to be a guest speaker at such an event especially if it is relevant to your offerings.

Social Events by a Company

Often these events can take form in the way that combines a light breakfast, brunch or lunch while presenting a training session or information seminar for one's products.

If the company has a conference room

It could be a venue

There are many other available venues that cater to this type of event so do your research.

Other Events

Often less formal entertaining events for suppliers and customers such as a company golf tournament or BBQ can be a very effective way to show appreciation for customer support and their business.

It also Builds Loyalty

By Showing Appreciation

As a sales representative, this will give you the opportunity to meet with clients on an informal basis and build a relationship.

They can also be a great relationship builder with your suppliers and become a great place for an informal customer/supplier meeting.

Personal Prospecting -DIY

Overview

This will probably your main source of leads if you work for one of the 80% who do not have or use a marketing plan. There may be some sort of advertising being done but it is usually not consistent or organized.

Usually you will get some secretarial back up for letters and proposals for your prospects. There could even be assistance in putting together some mailing campaigns.

If you are fortunate they will participate in some of the areas mentioned in the previous chapter.

For the Most Part

It will be like developing your own mini-marketing plan which is what we will be outlining here.

The following prospecting methods are primarily focused on what you; as the sales representative, will be doing.

Office Personnel

Leads from Your Office

Keep in close contact with your receptionist, order desk people, purchasing, shipping, your service department, and your engineering staff.

They are often the people who develop relationships with your customers and suppliers and will hear of projects, problems or needs that will benefit your efforts.

The Office Lead Source

Everyone in your company can become great sources for information on new projects. Get to know everyone in your company, because not only is everyone important; but, they could be a source for sales leads.

If they like the way you have treated them, and you have shown appreciation for the way they are assisting your customers, you have probably developed a great source for leads in your own company.

Your company support staff is usually in touch with your customers and suppliers monthly, weekly and sometimes they talk daily.

Often your office support staff will hear about projects sooner than you might from your own contacts. People like to talk and sometimes boast about their own company's progress.

These people are often on the inner circle of gossip and news in your industry. You will in turn hear about these projects often before they are announced publicly to the industry you are in.

Looking for a Good Person to take to lunch?

Try Someone in Your Company

Do it to show appreciation for working with you and your customers.

They will be happy to share information and leads if they like you and appreciate your demonstration of gratitude.

Remember that while you are getting commissions on your efforts, they do not see anything for their involvement in your commission earnings. (unless there is profit sharing)

Sometimes co-workers become jealous of your earnings especially if it has involved their assistance. Rewarding them when you are successful goes a long way to keep a harmonious working environment.

Rewarding for Help

Taking them out for lunches as well as other perks like tickets to sports events or other entertainment activities will go a long way in creating that extra effort from them.

Do not leave anyone out of the group that you work with

Pay for a night out dining at a local restaurant for them and their partner. Often, they may work late while their partner is waiting at home.

This Shows your Appreciation

For their Partners Understanding

Note: You need to be earning some serious commissions to begin doing this; and most of all, so you can keep this activity going.

Do not start and then stop. Do not go overboard. Maybe do a monthly thing for someone different each month.

Small and often, is better than, large an infrequent. Keep the perks similar in size for everyone.

Maybe do a Group thing for the Whole Office

Remember this can also be a tax write-off

Suppliers

Do not forget the people who supply you with products or services.

We will discuss this further in Peer Networking

Telephone Cold Calls

Calling Previously Selected People

This method is being affected by the changing attitudes of buyers. In today's business environment, many potential prospects do not want to be disturbed, unless they have made the first contact.

Make sure you have a good presentation as it is hard to get past the gate keepers.

If you are persistent this can often be a surprisingly good source for leads because fewer and fewer sales people are making cold calls on the telephone.

Make a list of places you can call when you have spare time. You can make your lists in none prime time or off hours and on weekends.

Always have 50 – 100 names of places complete with names and telephone numbers you can call. Set your minimum call list and Maintain it

Again, the law of numbers will produce some good appointments.

When Nothing else is Happening

Sit down and Make some Telephone Calls

Try This Approach

- Introduce yourself, your company and the product/service you are promoting.
- Ask if they have heard of you and if this is something that they would be interested in seeing or hearing about.
- If yes, make an appointment

If no Appointment can be made

- If they say no - ask them if you can send or drop off any information. If they still say no - thank them and hang up.

- If they say yes send me information, get their name and title.
- If you are not sure of the correct spelling of their name, call back and speak to the person on reception.
    - Say that you just talked to (name the person) and are sending or dropping off some literature for them.
    - Ask if you can get the correct spelling and proper title of that person?

Send your information and they will be eligible for a follow-up call to see if they got the information, have any questions or will make an appointment to see you.

Blogging (posting)

Blogging often provides commentary on a subject. Some will function as an online viewpoint on something in your industry. It could become an information source.

Others will perform more of an online branding source for a company, its offerings or even individuals within the company.

A typical blog may contain text, images, and links to other blogs, web pages or other media types related to its topic.

The ability of readers to leave comments is often part of many blogs.

Note: If you allow comments, there should be some type of screening process to eliminate public viewing of the unethical or obscene comments.

Often leaving some critical comments in, will show readers that this is an open forum. Often by doing this, you raise the overall level of reader trust.

If you develop a following they will become a great asset and good source of leads.

They will see you as an authority figure and want to read what you might to say about your industry, and even ask you to provide feedback and answers for their needs or problems.

If you Start a Blog

You must be consistent and establish a routine that works so people know when to expect your next post.

Choose a date that is easily identified; such as the last Friday of each month, the first and third Monday of every month or the 1st and 15th.

Establish it and Stick with it

Pace yourself and do not try to do more than you can easily handle.

Possibly keep a few previously prepared posts on file to use in an emergency when you do not have the time to do one.

In Word Press you can even schedule future posts over 3 – 4 months. This way you can plan a series and let things happen.

Post Office

If your employer will not provide this service, consider doing it yourself. It can pay big dividends if your products provide the right *Return on your Investment* of time and cost for materials.

a) News Letters to Past Contacts

A method that often works well is sending a monthly newsletter by the postal services directly to your past contacts who did not buy.

This becomes an excellent additional way of keeping a presence without the need of making continuous follow up phone calls.

Do not make the mistake of following up after such a mailing or you will defeat the purpose of this subtle informal contact.

Past Prospects do not feel threatened by postal newsletters; especially if they know there is no call coming after it.

They are not threatened because they can choose to read them or ignore them, and they know that you will be none the wiser.

After a while they may even look forward to them

A hard copy is more likely to get filed for future reference or circulated immediately. Often it will re-kindle someone's interest.

The main thing that happens here is that you keep your company and products/services in front of your past prospects, in an easy and non-intrusive way.

For them it's like getting a post card from an old acquaintance, so keep the newsletter short, informative and friendly.

We Suggest via Post Office

This is because often emails get deleted without even being looked at, because purchasers and management get so many of them. Once they are deleted they are gone forever.

Most often there is more chance of being seen, being circulated or being filed if it is hard copy.

Always present something different or new, along with your standard messages. Often something totally unrelated to your offerings will create buzz and a following.

Even something like recipes for salads, BBQ cooking, or desserts work well. A humorous story can often do more than promoting your own offerings.

Provide Valuable Information

Make sure that you include helpful industry related information as well, that they will want to keep this on file for future reference.

It is amazing how newsletters can rejuvenate lost sales or create renewed interest in a product or service.

With every newsletter our company sent out, we always experienced some sort of activity immediately following its distribution. It is more effective to leave the contact initiative in the hands of your prospect to call you.

Sometimes the timing was just not right when you last called, or maybe a project may have been indefinitely delayed and has just been put back on the front burner again.

Non-Prime Time

Sending newsletters is prospecting that can be done during non-prime time. Keep adding these non-prime time prospecting ways to your off hours prospecting potential.

Build your Lists. You need to keep as many active contacts as possible and distribute the newsletters on a regular schedule. When any name is no longer valid find out who replaced them.

This is an Excellent Way

Of Renewing Possibilities, as well

b) News Letters to Existing Customers

Existing customers can be great references and can become prospects for new business. Your company has gained their trust and respect, or they would not be customers.

Send the same style of newsletter addressed, stuffed and with a stamp for postal delivery. Do it as you did for non-customers. Part of the best Sales Prospecting is Mining your own Satisfied Customers.

Have a different grouping and format of information that is specifically sent to your existing customers. Thank them for their business. Inform them of important events in your company, or the industry.

Become a source of news, and you will keep everyone's attention, and support. They will also talk about you to others in a positive way.

There is a follow up for your newsletter with existing customers and it is a little different.

Often an informal in-person drop in call immediately following distribution of a newsletter, is demonstrating just good plain customer appreciation.

Make it a business/social visit to see if your company is looking after them. A newsletter and visit after can often lead to a new sale or prospect referral.

c) News Letters to Suppliers

Do not forget about your Suppliers. They are an extension of your contacts and will expand your reach.

They are people who have a vested interest in seeing your company successful because it will mean more sales for them. Here make your key contact(s) the recipient of the postal hard copy.

Emailing

News Letters

Many people read and prefer emails as a source of contact, so do not ignore this method. Do it along with your post office mailings of your newsletters, not as an either/or choice.

News Letters can easily be incorporated into an automated mailing service (auto-responders) that we mentioned earlier.

Use your automated email service to send out multiple copies of your electronic news letters to others in the same companies who you have met or worked with.

Sending a copy to everyone by post office would become very expensive.

Easier to Include Everyone

Many additional people will play a part in any decision making for your offerings. In this way, they do not feel that they have been left out of the loop and will be more prepared to support your cause.

People React Favorably to Being Remembered

This also really works well if your company has multiple products that will appeal to different departments. Usually your prospects have many people who can influence the purchasing of your offerings.

There is no cost to send the additional emails and therefore no excuse not to send them.

Group Emailing

Separate your emailing into different groups as some emailing could be more specific and for a group or several specified groups.

We have listed four groups as an example. Further groups can be made depending on your products or services.

The Four Groups

1) Past Contacts and Non-Customers

Send an email to the main contact as well as the extended contacts you may have worked with to try to obtain their business. This is very good for extending your influence as well.

2) Existing Customers

Sending email newsletters to office managers, plant managers, department heads as well as engineering, key plant and office people, maintenance people, shipping and receiving is like mining in pure gold.

You can get many of these email addresses from your own company staff and your main customer contact.

3) Suppliers

Do not forget about emailing your suppliers. Again, they have reasons for wanting to see you successful.

Sending email newsletters to their office managers, plant managers, department heads as well as engineering, key plant and office people, maintenance people, shipping and receiving is also like mining in pure gold.

You can also get many of these email addresses from your own company staff or your supplier contact.

4) Your Own Company

Never forget your own group of co-workers. They above all may appreciate being noticed and possibly even mentioned and thanked in your emails or newsletters.

Summary of Emailing

The greatest part about emailing is that it is virtually free. Along with building your initial lists you will need to keep it up to date and keep adding wherever you can.

Do not ignore this method of Prospecting as it allows you to reach these sources in an instant through your automated emailing service.

There is no paper cost, no printing costs, and no mailing costs – just your time spent. Yes, there is usually a small monthly service fee for the auto-responder but when the results are reviewed, it is very low.

What Other Method

Could be more Efficient and Cost Effective

And Environmentally Friendly as Well

Customers Referrals

Referrals will materialize, if you have serviced your customer well, and provided the confidence level that will usually be required for them to provide your name to others.

It takes a little more for them to provide names of referrals to you instead of just passing it on and allowing the people to contact you.

When they provide you with the name, it will mean you have been successful in building a substantial amount of trust.

The only way you can really prepare yourself for this type of lead, is to look after every client to the best of your ability. Most times you will need to ask for referrals even with a high level of customer trust.

Social Visits

Drop into existing or past customers whenever you are in their area.

It is amazing how one of these unannounced – *"Hi how you are drop-in calls"* - can make your customer feel appreciated.

Yes, a Social visit

Show interest, ask how things are going, and share industry information. This will be more of a social visit than a sales call.

We Stress a Social vs. Sales Approach

Say hi how you are or how are things going? How is the family? Wait for an answer. Maybe have a short discussion updating recent business and personal activities, and then be on your way. If they are busy just leave your card.

Such visits can be an excellent source of leads. While you are there; if the opportunity presents itself, it never hurts to ask if they know of anyone else who could use your product or services.

Do Not make it the Reason for your Call

Occasionally you may find out that they are expanding themselves or are having problems with other competitor's products and may need your assistance.

This can lead to supplying new offerings or more of your existing products or services. You will be surprised by the business that can come from a social visit.

Achievements - Birthdays - Seasons Greetings

Achievements

Often a company will achieve something special or reach a milestone such as 25th anniversary. Show your interest in the customer by dropping by or sending a congratulatory letter, card or gift.

Birthdays

Individuals like to be noticed. If you know that it is someone's birthday, send or drop off a card. Keep a list of your client's birthdays or special anniversaries if you can.

Show that you care, and it will be appreciated. Keep adding to your list.

Season's Greetings

Drop by existing and past customers during the December holiday season. It will make them feel good and important to be remembered and appreciated.

Maybe leave a small gift for the office like a small cheese platter or chocolates. Not too large to upset any rules or not too small or you will appear cheap.

Your appreciation, friendship and interest in how well they are doing, will come back many times over.

Do it mainly as a thank you and a call expressing appreciation for their past business. The act of kindness and gratitude will not go unnoticed or unappreciated by their office staff as well.

Peer Networking

One of the best ways for getting good sales leads is by establishing contact with non-competing sales and service people in other companies, who are calling on the same type of companies as you are.

Peer Sources for Networking

- Your own suppliers are great sources for peer networking and they have a vested interest in your success.
- Your co-workers in your office and their contacts
- Other non-competitive sales people servicing your industry
- Owners and managers of your customers.

In my most successful selling years, my suppliers provided me with over 80% of my leads that developed into sales.

They also became the recipients of leads from me. Even better they also shared in the business obtained by supplying their products for my projects.

If your lead source is a supplier that your new prospect trusts and respects, it is perhaps the most powerful and qualified lead you can get.

Begin Building Right Away

When starting out, unless you already have friends and contacts in the industry, peer networking will take time to develop.

Start building your own network as soon as you can and keep building throughout your entire career.

Where to Find Them

You will meet your peers at trade shows, seminars, conferences, social activities, and often when attending a joint project meeting held by your own suppliers or even customers.

To increase lead sources, ask your customer who supplies them with other products that are non-competitive to you. You can then develop them as a lead source.

You could say: *"I often am asked who I might recommend for (*name the product*). If you are happy with your source, would it be possible to get their name and number so that I might contact them to establish a relationship.*

Once you get a Name

Call that person and Introduce Yourself

Tell them where you got their name. Meet with them for a coffee and discuss how you can help each other. They are also looking for contacts to network with, so this is usually not difficult.

Make sure the lead source is reliable and is respected, because you will be mentioning their name to your customers.

Some Pointers

Many people will already have contacts with whom they network, so it may take some time to win their confidence.

Sometimes the loyalty of a peer is attached to where they get the most benefits, like leads or spin off sales.

Be aware of Where their Loyalty lies

The best way is to start building peer lead sources; is to be the first to provide leads to them, for their offerings. Be careful at first, build the relationship slowly, until you are sure you can trust them.

You do not want them to take your important contacts to your competition. Provide some smaller leads first and wait and see how they handle them.

When you finally break the barrier, and get a lead from them, make sure you thank them, and do the best that you can to justify their gesture of good faith.

Look after Their Prospect Well

Get permission to use the name of your lead source, or even better, have them introduce you personally.

Servicing Leads

This is not something to take lightly, because you will only be judged by the results of the last lead you handled. Nothing will make a lead source disappear faster than, not looking after their lead properly.

This is called networking, so always be prepared to always keep doing the same in return, or this method will soon dry up.

Nourish it; Stick with it even though it takes a while to develop. When it is done right; in my opinion, the return your invested time beats every other type of leads sourcing.

Peer Networking is always About

Building and Maintaining Trust.

Peer networking is one of the most powerful introductions to a potential client. It is also like mining pure gold, and there is nothing better for your success.

Social Networking

There is another form of networking that many people use to obtain clients. It is referred to as social networking. It occurs usually during lunch time, after hours during the week, and often weekends.

Some sales people look for different social functions where they may attend and meet potential prospects or lead sources. Others may join organizations such as Chamber of Commerce or associations related to their industry.

It could be a trade show for other products, an exhibit or anywhere you mingle and meet people. It could be a supplier golf tournament or benefit.

Usually at these events, people tend to relax and let their guard down. They talk about their families, their hobbies and what they do in their spare time.

Often friendships are generated and continued in the workplace. Some will become customers or lead sources and even lifelong friends.

Always Behave at an Acceptable Level.

Party Animals get their Attention but Rarely get the Business

Cold Calling in Person

a) Extra time when in the Area

When you are out seeing the prospects that you have made appointments with, you will often find yourself with extra time especially if there is a cancellation or a call ends quickly.

Always carry plenty of promotional material to leave with other companies in the area.

Yes, we did say cold calling does not work. But in this case, we are not going to try to see anyone. We are just leaving information, getting a name (if possible) and telephone number to call back. It is cold calling with a twist.

Be Resourceful

Many sales people get angry at a no show, or a shorter than expected no-results-meeting. They do not take advantage of the extra time that has unexpectedly become available.

They go for a coffee or early lunch or may head back to the office or even home, instead of using this BONUS time and continuing to work at getting prospects while in the area.

Surprisingly; unplanned cold calling like this, can pay off big. Every potential prospect uncovered, is one that you would not have otherwise obtained.

In addition, you still have the original prospect to contact again later.

The Approach

When you make this type of cold call:

You say *"I was making a call at (your call) and I noticed your company and I was wondering what your company does?*

If it appears like someone who could use your offerings:

You say *"I do not have time to see anyone right now; but, could I drop off some information about our company.*

If they say Yes

You continue: *"May I ask who I would speak to about (whatever your offerings are) when I do my follow up."*

Try and get a name then leave

Do not try to get in to see the person! Even if you did manage to see the prospect, people do not like this type of interruption without an appointment. It will affect future attempts to see them.

This low-key Approach

Is far more Effective in the long run

If you do not get a name when you are there check any directories you may have, or on line. Follow up the next day and ask for that person.

You say: *"Yesterday I left information for the person that looks after (your Product). Who I would ask for when I call for an appointment?"*

If you get a name, ask*: "Do they have a title?"*

Once you have a name, the prospect is now eligible for a follow up telephone call.

b) Targeted Companies (visual signs)

This Type of approach is a planned and targeted one. Companies who may use your offerings will sometimes show visible signs that you can see from outside.

Some Examples

- If you sell liquid paint for industrial spraying equipment, it might be as easy as looking for factories that have exhaust stacks to remove contaminants from their building.
    - Paint stacks are usually identifiable and distinct.
- Other types of exhaust stacks could mean a company that is welding and would be a prospect for welding equipment and supplies.
- Exhaust stacks could also mean a potential need for air make up units.
- Even the company name will usually tell you what they do. You can Google the name on your phone and find out while you are in the area.

When you approach the receptionist, (if there is one) ask if they do any kind of welding, or painting or whatever the process is that needs your offerings.

You Say: *"I was just making a call down the street and noticed the exhaust stacks on your roof."*

Using the type of offering you have as the example

You ask: "Would your company do any (your example).

If they say yes

You say *"I do not have time to see anyone right now; but, could I drop off some information about our company.*

Continue: *"May I ask who I would speak to about (your offerings) when I do my follow up."*

Try and get a Name and then Leave.

Do not try to get in to see the person! Even if you did manage to see the prospect, people do not like this type of interruption without an appointment.

Just like example a) this low-key approach

Is far more effective in the long run

If you do not get a name when you are there check any directories you may have, or on line. Follow up the next day and ask for that person. If you do not get a name, Call the next day.

You say: *"Yesterday I left information for the person that looks after (your Product). Who I would ask for when I call for an appointment?"*

If you get a name, ask: *"Do they have a title?"*

Once you have a name, the prospect is now eligible for a follow up telephone call. Do this cold call approach whenever you can, and this extra time could allow 3 or 4 calls and maybe the discovery of a new prospect.

You will learn the Signs or Type of Companies to Look for

Trade Shows as a Visitor

If you are not fortunate to have your company participate as an exhibitor in a trade show for your business type or industry, do the next best thing.

Become Visible as a VISITOR

Network with all your peers and leave information with potential prospects.

Opportunities may be characterized as silver or second best as compared to an exhibitor; but, participating as a visitor is still a great source for prospects.

You can socialize with existing peers and obtaining new peer net-workers.

Make sure your approaches are non-intrusive and do not interrupt the exhibitor's opportunities to speak with their own potential clients.

Approach them Only if

They are Not Engaged in a Conversation.

If you are talking when a prospect approaches them, politely step back or leave. Come back again if it is appropriate.

Prospecting Summary

The To-Do and Not-To-Do List

Do Follow up - One important thing that you should be doing in all forms of prospecting is following up. If you have obtained a name and you have not yet called that potential client, follow it up.

This backlog often happens after a trade show, where there can be so many leads obtained at once. Often a form of thank you for visiting our booth is a good beginning. It acts as a reminder as well.

There is no point in taking the time or incurring the cost to get a name, and then not use it. Having a huge list of potential clients remains just that, until you make the call, to turn them into a viable prospect.

The worst thing that can happen is that they can say NO we are no longer interested. It is more important to get a no and remove it from your list, than to leave the approach unfinished.

Thinking about your uncalled leads and feeling guilty can drag you down quicker than the No's you might get.

Failure to Follow up

Many people fail to follow up. These names are the most important part of prospecting, but they are of no value unless you use them.

The effectiveness of a lead diminishes very soon after it has been provided, so do not wait too long to follow up or the opportunity will be gone.

Do - Find what prospecting methods work best for you.

Find five or six methods that suit your personality and offerings. Use them constantly.

Be creative when sending or dropping off information. Provide something that will catch their attention and arouse their interest and cause them to call or check you out on your web site.

Do Smile - Show Enthusiasm and the Right Attitude. Smile when you talk on the phone. Do this, and it will be transmitted to the person at the other end. The smile when talking to a person is always felt.

Be Enthusiastic - It is one of the greatest tools you can use, and it is contagious. The more enthused you are, the more enthused will be your prospect. Always keep enthusiasm present.

Norman Vincent Peale once said: *"Enthusiasm releases the drive to carry you over obstacles and adds significance to all you do."*

Do See the Right Person - Every product or service is usually handled by a similar type of position in any company.

- If it is office supplies you are selling, it is usually the office manager who buys.
- Repeat plant supplies are most often handled by a purchasing agent.
- You might see the production manager or general manager if you are introducing new products for their manufacturing process.

The people who do the day-to-day purchasing are often "not" the ones who will select your new product.

Find out who all the people involved in making those decisions to make a change are. Your own experience will soon teach you who these people usually are.

Talk to your manager and ask who it was that they initially contacted when presenting their product or service to your existing customers.

This will usually be enough to get you started until your own experience takes over.

Do not leave people out - If you are seeing a decision maker who is completely different than the person that does the day-to-day ordering, do not leave the day-to-day person out of the dialogue.

Most often, they will have two or three accepted sources for the same products or services. If you alienate them; even though you are shown as a source, they could ignore you or could undermine your future sales possibilities.

Do not - Use prospecting methods you dislike - Do not use a prospecting method that makes you uncomfortable, or you hate doing because you will rarely be successful, and your attitude will come across to the customer.

Do not Rely on Just One Method, or you will usually come up short. Use more than the top four or five to avoid lowering your chances for success. Alternate them for variety and results.

Often your enthusiasm for one type will diminish over time. Make a change and re-charge the enthusiasm.

Overlap types of prospecting by employing those that are productive during prime time in the day and using others that can be done after hours.

Use as Many Prospecting Methods

That can be done in your Spare Time

Your Approach

Getting an Appointment

Prospect Makes First Contact

In most cases where your company is doing the marketing and in many areas of your own prospecting, the methods have been designed to have the prospect make first contact. In these cases, the appointment setting is a lot easier.

You will simply call

- Introduce yourself and your company.
- Thank them for the inquiry regarding (whatever it is).
- Refer to where the lead came from if you can.
- Qualify and get the details on what they were asking about
- Set an appointment to see them.

Example:

You Say: *"Which day would be best for you to see me – Tuesday or Wednesday".* If they agree to a day, ask which is best "morning or afternoon?" Next set the time "Would time A or time B be best for you?

Thank them and repeat the arranged time: "Thank you, we will see you next Wednesday afternoon at 2:30.

Perhaps they will request sending the information for them to review before your visit and that is often good.

They are more prepared for your visit and are a better prospect as well because they are familiar with your offerings.

Important

- Make sure you have the correct spelling of their name, proper title and the company mailing address.

- If you do not already have their email address, ask for it and if you can send information this way for immediate viewing. This quick response keeps the interest level high.
- Do not try to make a follow up appointment now because they have already indicated they are interested. Let them review the material.
- Tell them you will call in a few days; if you have not heard from them, to see if they have any questions.
- Calling to answer questions is not intrusive.
- Follow up in the agreed time frame and ask if they have any questions. Answer them if there are any.
- Now you can ask for an appointment.

You Make First Contact

When you are making the first personal contact, make your verbal approach as professional as you can. Practice until it is automatic, but not boring.

a) Leads from Peers

When you call the person that an outside source has told you about, introduce yourself and your company.

You can say: *"I was speaking to (Dave from X Company) about your company and asked who I should speak with concerning (your offerings), and he gave me your name."*

"Are you the right person to speak to?"

If they are not the right person, ask who it is. If they are the right person or when you talk to the right person:

You can then say: *"I will be in your area next week and would like to drop off some information for you to look at,"*

"If you are available when I call it would take 10 – 15 minutes to quickly explain our products/services to you, and then I will be on my way."

Wait for their reply

If they say "OK", make the appointment and set a time. Thank them, repeat the scheduled time, and then say you are looking forward to meeting them.

If they are not interested in an appointment, ask if you can drop the information off next week when you are in the area for them to look at when they have time.

Then say you will call a few days after to see if they have any questions. Again, do not try to make a follow up appointment at this time as they have already said no.

Calling to see if there are questions will set up the opportunity to ask for an appointment.

b) Cold Calling by Telephone

When you call, introduce yourself and your company to the person answering.

If you do not have a Name

You may start by asking: *"With whom should I speak to about (your offerings)?"*

OR

You might say: *"I understand that your company does a lot of welding".*

> *"If I wanted to show my products to the person who will specify the source for welding supplies that you use, may I ask who that would, be?"*

If you get a name, ask if they are available to talk to

If they are not available, ask if they have an extension for future contact purposes?

Call later and ask for them by name

Or by extension, if you have it.

When you get through to that person

- Introduce yourself, your company and what your offerings are.
- Qualify them and if there are possibilities, continue
- Say that you will be making some calls in their area (whenever) and would they have 10 – 15 minutes to speak to you about (your offerings)?

Wait for their reply, **if they say** "OK", make the appointment. Thank them, repeat the scheduled time, and then say you are looking forward to meeting them.

If they are not interested in an appointment, ask if you can drop the information off next week when you are in the area for them to look at when they have time.

Then say you will call a few days after to see if they have any questions. Again, do not try to make a follow up appointment at this time as they have already said no.

Calling to see if there are questions

Will provide the Opportunity to ask for an appointment

c) Customer Referrals

When you call, you will already have a name from your customer.

Introduce yourself and your company and say: *"Company X is a good customer of ours and is very happy with our (offerings).*

(Say the person's name) suggested that I should call you to see if we might show you (what you offer).

Say that you will be making some calls in their area (*next week or whenever*) and would they have 10 – 15 minutes to speak to you about (your offerings)?

Wait for their reply, if they say "OK" - Make the appointment. Thank them, repeat the scheduled time, and then say you are looking forward to meeting them.

If they are not interested in an appointment, ask if you can drop the information off next week when you are in the area for them to look at when they have time.

Then say you will call a few days after to see if they have any questions. Again, do not try to make a follow up appointment at this time as they have already said no.

Calling to see if there are questions will set up the opportunity to ask for an appointment.

d) Pre-Planned In-Person Cold Calling

This is cold calling in person with a twist. You are not trying to see anyone. You are doing this to set the reason for your next call and too get a name. If there is a reception area introduce yourself and say:

The approach "I was making some calls in the area and your (company name, materials outside, exhaust stacks, find something) suggested to me that your company might be interested in (whatever your offerings are).

Finish with: *"I do not have any time to see anyone right now and I realize that it is best to make an appointment, so I would just like to leave some literature for whoever might take care of this area. Would that be alright?* ***If they say yes***

You Ask: *"Who would I ask for when I call for an appointment?"*

Note: If there is just a telephone in the lobby call the reception and say the same as above. Make sure at the end for either way, that you have all the information you will need for follow up.

SUMMARY

Prospecting is your Avenue for Success.

If it is part of your job, and you are good at it, you will have the keys to achieve all your sales goals. This part 5 has provided you with some of the tools and the ways to find your prospects, future customers and clients.

Start with these and Always Be Building

If you know how to create your own leads, you will always have a large inventory of potential customers and opportunities for sales.

Even if your employer supplies leads, you should learn the methods outlined in this book. Prospecting is a skill set that will always be of enormous value in applying for any sales position.

Without this skill set you will remain unable to be self-reliant in your undertakings as a sales person. Without this ability, you will always need others to create opportunities for you.

Selling should be all about setting your own goals, creating your own future and pathway to success.

By learning and mastering the information in this book you will indeed become self-reliant and a self-starter.

That's What the Direct Sales Profession

Is All About

Wayne E Shillum - Author

END OF PART FIVE

www.ingramcontent.com/pod-product-compliance
Ingram Content Group UK Ltd.
Pitfield, Milton Keynes, MK11 3LW, UK
UKHW051129260726
13967UKWH00010B/2942